KB018050

영어 성경
100일 필사 노트

구성 펜앤페이퍼 Pen&Paper

읽는 일과 쓰는 일을 하는 출판기획 모임입니다.
책읽기의 즐거움과 손글씨 감성을 함께 느낄 수 있는 책들을 기획하고 있습니다.
쓴 책으로는 《영어 필기체 10일 완성 노트》, 《영어 필기체 100일 기적의 노트》,
《어린 왕자 영어 필기체 100일 필사 노트》, 《음악이 있는 팝송 영어 필사》가 있습니다.

영어 성경 100일 필사 노트

1판 1쇄 인쇄 2024년 1월 5일
1판 1쇄 발행 2024년 1월 15일
—
구성 펜앤페이퍼
—
펴낸이 김은중
편집 허선영 디자인 김순수
펴낸곳 가위바위보
출판 등록 2020년 11월 17일 제 2020-000316호
주소 경기도 부천시 소향로 25, 511호 (우편번호 14544)
팩스 02-6008-5011 전자우편 gbbbooks@naver.com
네이버블로그 gbbbooks 인스타그램 gbbbooks 페이스북 gbbbooks
—
ISBN 979-11-92156-24-8 13740

* 책값은 뒤표지에 있습니다.
* 이 책의 내용을 사용하려면 반드시 저작권자와 출판사의 동의를 얻어야 합니다.
* 잘못된 책은 구입처에서 바꿔 드립니다.

가위바위보 출판사는 나답게 만드는 책, 그리고 다함께 즐기는 책을 만듭니다.

영어 성경

The Bible

100일 필사 노트

GBB

지혜롭게 살아가도록 돕는
하나님의 말씀을 새기며 사랑을 느끼는 100일

성경은 오래된 지혜이며 하나님의 말씀입니다. 그래서 많은 사람들이 성경을 읽고 묵상하며 지혜를 얻습니다. 여러분은 어떻게 성경을 읽고 있나요? 눈으로 읽기, 소리 내어 읽기, 함께 읽기 등 여러 방법이 있겠지만 가장 능동적이고 적극적으로 성경을 읽는 방법은 바로 손으로 직접 쓰면서 읽는 필사입니다. 성경 필사 시간은 내가 하나님을 찾고, 하나님이 주시는 사랑을 충만하게 느낄 수 있는 은혜의 시간이지요.

성경을 영어로 읽고 써보고 싶은 분들도 계실 거예요. 영어 성경이 어렵게 번역된 우리말 성경보다 성경 원문의 의미를 더 이해하기 쉽다는 말도 있지요. 하지만 영어 성경 전문을 다 완독하기에는 부담스럽고 막막하게 느껴질 수 있답니다.

《영어 성경 100일 필사 노트》는 영어 성경 읽기에 도전하고 싶은 분들을 위해 영어 성경 신약 편에서 뽑은 성경 구절을 100일 동안 영어로 필사할 수 있도록 만든 책입니다.

삶을 지혜롭게 살아가도록 돕는 성경 구절을 통해 100일 동안 오롯하게 하나님의 사랑을 느껴보길 바랍니다.

Contents
마스터한 날에 체크하세요

성경으로 하는 영어 필사

☆ 〈영어 성경〉 신약 편에서 뽑은 성경 구절

이 책에 수록된 성경 구절은 신약 편에서 뽑았어요. 영어 성경은 NIV(New International Version)를 사용했고, 한글 성경 구절은 개역개정 성경에서 발췌했습니다.

☆ 영어 필사의 흥미를 더해주는 필기체 수록

성경 구절을 여러 가지 서체로 써보세요. 영어 필사를 더 재미있고 즐겁게 할 수 있도록 필기체로도 쓸 수 있게 구성했으니, 자신의 영어 서체로 필사하거나 필기체로도 따라 써 보세요. 〈필기체 맛보기〉 코너가 연습해보는데 도움이 될 거예요. 다양한 방법으로 필사를 해보면 영어 필사의 색다른 매력을 만날 수 있답니다.

☆ 영어 공부도 할 수 있는 성경 필사

영어 성경 필사는 좋은 영어 공부법 중의 하나입니다. 모르는 단어나 문법이 나오면 사전을 찾아보면서 영어 공부도 겸해보세요. 넉넉하게 만든 노트 공간에 단어의 뜻과 예문을 적어보세요. 한글 성경 발췌문을 보고 뜻을 음미하면서 한글로 필사도 해보고요.

☆ 하나님의 말씀을 더 깊이 묵상할 수 있는 필사

필사를 한 다음에는 말씀이 내게 주시는 은혜에 대해 깊이 생각하는 묵상 시간도 꼭 가져 보세요. 묵상을 통해 얻은 깨달음을 적어도 좋겠지요.

☆ 좋아하는 성경 구절 필사

여러분이 좋아하는 성경 구절을 찾아 책의 마지막 쪽에 있는 〈좋아하는 성경 구절 쓰기〉 코너에 써보세요. '나만의 하나님의 말씀 기록장'이 만들어질 거예요.

The books of THE NEW TESTAMENT

Matthew 마태복음

Mark 마가복음

Luke 누가복음

John 요한복음

Acts 사도행전

Romans 로마서

1 Corinthians 고린도전서

2 Corinthians 고린도후서

Galatians 갈라디아서

Ephesians 에베소서

Philippians 빌립보서

Colossians 골로새서

1 Thessalonians 데살로니가전서

2 Thessalonians 데살로니가후서

1 Timothy 디모데전서

2 Timothy 디모데후서

Titus 디도서

Philemon 빌레몬서

Hebrews 히브리서

James 야고보서

1 Peter 베드로전서

2 Peter 베드로후서

1 John 요한1서

2 John 요한2서

3 John 요한3서

Jude 유다서

Revelation 요한계시록

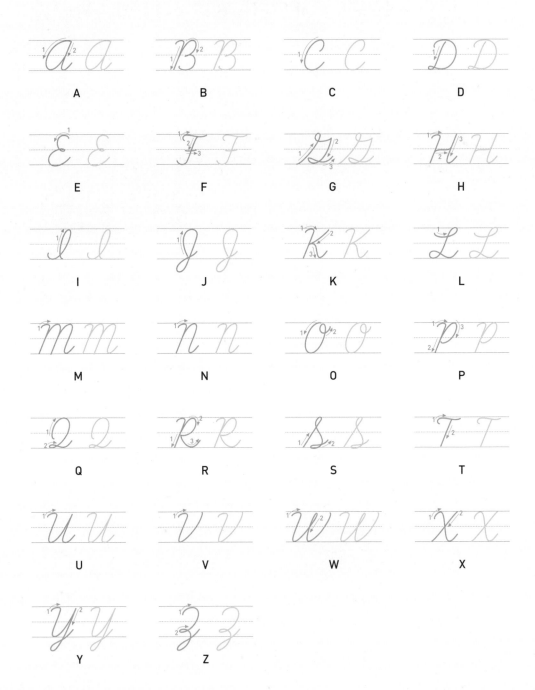

A   B   C   D

E   F   G   H

I   J   K   L

M   N   O   P

Q   R   S   T

U   V   W   X

Y   Z

Small Letters 필기체 소문자

a

b

c

d

e

f

g

h

i

j

k

l

m

n

o

p

q

r

s

t

u

v

w

x

y

z

ABCDEFGHIJKLMNOPQRSTUVWXYZ

ABCDEFGHIJKLMNOPQRSTUVWXYZ

ABCDEFGHIJKLMNOPQRSTUVWXYZ

Tip i, j, t, x의 점과 선은 마지막에 쓰세요.

abcdefghijklmnopqrstuvwxyz

abcdefghijklmnopqrstuvwxyz

abcdefghijklmnopqrstuvwxyz

• 마태복음·마가복음에서 뽑은 성경 구절

DAY 1

Jesus answered, "It is written: 'Man shall not live on bread alone, but on every word that comes from the mouth of God.'" Matthew 4:4

Jesus answered, "It is written: 'Man shall not live on bread alone, but on every word that comes from the mouth of God.'"

예수께서 대답하여 이르시되 기록되었으되 사람이 떡으로만 살 것이 아니요
하나님의 입으로부터 나오는 모든 말씀으로 살 것이라 하였느니라 하시니
마태복음 4:4

You are the salt of the earth. But if the salt loses its saltiness, how can it be made salty again? It is no longer good for anything, except to be thrown out and trampled underfoot. Matthew 5:13

You are the salt of the earth. But if the salt loses its saltiness, how can it be made salty again? It is no longer good for anything, except to be thrown out and trampled underfoot.

너희는 세상의 소금이니 소금이 만일 그 맛을 잃으면 무엇으로 짜게 하리요
후에는 아무 쓸 데 없어 다만 밖에 버려져 사람에게 밟힐 뿐이니라
마태복음 5:13

In the same way, let your light shine before others, that they may see your good deeds and glorify your Father in heaven. Matthew 5:16

In the same way, let your light shine before others, that they may see your good deeds and glorify your Father in heaven.

이같이 너희 빛이 사람 앞에 비치게 하여 그들로 너희 착한 행실을 보고 하늘에 계신 너희 아버지께 영광을 돌리게 하라 마태복음 5:16

But I tell you, love your enemies and pray for those who persecute you, that you may be children of your Father in heaven. Matthew 5:44-45

But I tell you, love your enemies and pray for those who persecute you, that you may be children of your Father in heaven.

나는 너희에게 이르노니 너희 원수를 사랑하며 너희를 박해하는 자를 위하여 기도하라
이같이 한즉 하늘에 계신 너희 아버지의 아들이 되리니 마태복음 5:44-45

But when you give to the needy, do not let your left hand know what your right hand is doing, so that your giving may be in secret. Then your Father, who sees what is done in secret, will reward you. Matthew 6 : 3-4

But when you give to the needy, do not let your left hand know what your right hand is doing, so that your giving may be in secret. Then your Father, who sees what is done in secret, will reward you.

너는 구제할 때에 오른손이 하는 것을 왼손이 모르게 하여
네 구제함을 은밀하게 하라
은밀한 중에 보시는 너의 아버지께서 갚으시리라 마태복음 6:3-4

DAY 6

No one can serve two masters. Either you will hate the one and love the other, or you will be devoted to the one and despise the other. You cannot serve both God and money. Matthew 6:24

No one can serve two masters. Either you

will hate the one and love the other, or

you will be devoted to the one and despise

the other. You cannot serve both God and

money.

한 사람이 두 주인을 섬기지 못할 것이니 혹 이를 미워하고
저를 사랑하거나 혹 이를 중히 여기고 저를 경히 여김이라
너희가 하나님과 재물을 겸하여 섬기지 못하느니라 마태복음 6:24

Therefore do not worry about tomorrow, for tomorrow will worry about itself. Each day has enough trouble of its own. Matthew 6:34

Therefore do not worry about tomorrow, for tomorrow will worry about itself. Each day has enough trouble of its own.

그러므로 내일 일을 위하여 염려하지 말라 내일 일은 내일이 염려할 것이요
한 날의 괴로움은 그 날로 족하니라 마태복음 6:34

Come to me, all you who are weary and burdened, and I will give you rest. Matthew 11:28

Come to me, all you who are weary and

burdened, and I will give you rest.

수고하고 무거운 짐 진 자들아 다 내게로 오라 내가 너희를 쉬게 하리라
마태복음 11:28

DAY 9

Take my yoke upon you and learn from me, for I am gentle and humble in heart, and you will find rest for your souls. For my yoke is easy and my burden is light. Matthew 11:29-30

Take my yoke upon you and learn from me,

for I am gentle and humble in heart, and

you will find rest for your souls. For my

yoke is easy and my burden is light.

나는 마음이 온유하고 겸손하니 나의 멍에를 메고 내게 배우라
그리하면 너희 마음이 쉼을 얻으리니
이는 내 멍에는 쉽고 내 짐은 가벼움이라 하시니라 마태복음 11:29-30

Therefore go and make disciples of all nations, baptizing them in the name of the Father and of the Son and of the Holy Spirit, and teaching them to obey everything I have commanded you. And surely I am with you always, to the very end of the age. Matthew 28:19-20

Therefore go and make disciples of all nations,

baptizing them in the name of the Father

and of the Son and of the Holy Spirit, and

teaching them to obey everything I have

commanded you. And surely I am with you

always, to the very end of the age.

그러므로 너희는 가서 모든 민족을 제자로 삼아 아버지와 아들과 성령의 이름으로 세례를 베풀고 내가 너희에게 분부한 모든 것을 가르쳐 지키게 하라 볼지어다 내가 세상 끝날까지 너희와 항상 함께 있으리라 하시니라 마태복음 28:19-20

"The time has come," he said. "The kingdom of God has come near. Repent and believe the good news!"

Mark 1:15

"The time has come," he said. "The kingdom of God has come near. Repent and believe the good news!"

이르시되 때가 찼고 하나님의 나라가 가까이 왔으니
회개하고 복음을 믿으라 하시더라 마가복음 1:15

On hearing this, Jesus said to them, "It is not the healthy who need a doctor, but the sick. I have not come to call the righteous, but sinners." Mark 2:17

On hearing this, Jesus said to them, "It is not the healthy who need a doctor, but the sick. I have not come to call the righteous, but sinners."

예수께서 들으시고 그들에게 이르시되 건강한 자에게는
의사가 쓸 데 없고 병든 자에게라야 쓸 데 있느니라
나는 의인을 부르러 온 것이 아니요 죄인을 부르러 왔노라 하시니라
마가복음 2:17

And no one pours new wine into old wineskins. Otherwise, the wine will burst the skins, and both the wine and the wineskins will be ruined. No, they pour new wine into new wineskins. Mark 2:22

And no one pours new wine into old wineskins. Otherwise, the wine will burst the skins, and both the wine and the wineskins will be ruined. No, they pour new wine into new wineskins.

새 포도주를 낡은 가죽 부대에 넣는 자가 없나니 만일 그렇게 하면
새 포도주가 부대를 터뜨려 포도주와 부대를 버리게 되리라
오직 새 포도주는 새 부대에 넣느니라 마가복음 2:22

Others, like seed sown on good soil, hear the word, accept it, and produce a crop-some thirty, some sixty, some a hundred times what was sown. Mark 4:20

Others, like seed sown on good soil, hear the

word, accept it, and produce a crop-some

thirty, some sixty, some a hundred times

what was sown.

좋은 땅에 뿌려졌다는 것은 곧 말씀을 듣고 받아 삼십 배나 육십 배나 백 배의 결실을 하는 자니라
마가복음 4:20

He said to her, "Daughter, your faith has healed you.
Go in peace and be freed from your suffering." Mark 5:34

He said to her, "Daughter, your faith has

healed you. Go in peace and be freed from

your suffering."

예수께서 이르시되 딸아 네 믿음이 너를 구원하였으니 평안히 가라 네 병에서 놓여 건강할지어다
마가복음 5:34

Because they all saw him and were terrified. Immediately he spoke to them and said, "Take courage! It is I. Don't be afraid." Mark 6:50

Because they all saw him and were terrified.

Immediately he spoke to them and said, "Take

courage! It is I. Don't be afraid."

그들이 다 예수를 보고 놀람이라 이에 예수께서 곧 그들에게 말씀하여 이르시되
안심하라 내니 두려워하지 말라 하시고 마가복음 6:50

Sitting down, Jesus called the Twelve and said,
"Anyone who wants to be first must be the very last,
and the servant of all." Mark 9 :35

Sitting down, Jesus called the Twelve and said, "Anyone who wants to be first must be the very last, and the servant of all."

예수께서 앉으사 열두 제자를 불러서 이르시되
누구든지 첫째가 되고자 하면 뭇 사람의 끝이 되며
뭇 사람을 섬기는 자가 되어야 하리라 하시고 마가복음 9:35

Whoever welcomes one of these little children in my name welcomes me; and whoever welcomes me does not welcome me but the one who sent me. Mark 9:37

Whoever welcomes one of these little children

in my name welcomes me; and whoever

welcomes me does not welcome me but the

one who sent me.

누구든지 내 이름으로 이런 어린 아이 하나를 영접하면 곧 나를 영접함이요
누구든지 나를 영접하면 나를 영접함이 아니요 나를 보내신 이를 영접함이니라
마가복음 9:37

Jesus looked at them and said, "With man this is impossible, but not with God; all things are possible with God." Mark 10:27

Jesus looked at them and said, "With man this is impossible, but not with God; all things are possible with God."

예수께서 그들을 보시며 이르시되 사람으로는 할 수 없으되
하나님으로는 그렇지 아니하니 하나님으로서는 다 하실 수 있느니라
마가복음 10:27

Truly I tell you, if anyone says to this mountain, 'Go, throw yourself into the sea,' and does not doubt in their heart but believes that what they say will happen, it will be done for them. Mark 11:23

Truly I tell you, if anyone says to this

mountain, ' Go, throw yourself into the sea,'

and does not doubt in their heart but believes

that what they say will happen, it will be

done for them.

내가 진실로 너희에게 이르노니 누구든지 이 산더러 들리어 바다에 던져지라 하며
그 말하는 것이 이루어질 줄 믿고 마음에 의심하지 아니하면 그대로 되리라 마가복음 11:23

• 누가복음·요한복음에서 뽑은 성경 구절

John answered them all, "I baptize you with water. But one who is more powerful than I will come, the straps of whose sandals I am not worthy to untie. He will baptize you with the Holy Spirit and fire." Luke 3:16

John answered them all, "I baptize you with

water. But one who is more powerful than

I will come, the straps of whose sandals I

am not worthy to untie. He will baptize you

with the Holy Spirit and fire."

요한이 모든 사람에게 대답하여 이르되 나는 물로 너희에게 세례를 베풀거니와
나보다 능력이 많으신 이가 오시나니 나는 그의 신발끈을 풀기도 감당하지 못하겠노라
그는 성령과 불로 너희에게 세례를 베푸실 것이요 누가복음 3:16

Blessed are you who are poor, for yours is the kingdom of God.

Blessed are you who hunger now, for you will be satisfied.

Blessed are you who weep now, for you will laugh.

Luke 6:20-21

Blessed are you who are poor, for yours is

the kingdom of God.

Blessed are you who hunger now, for you

will be satisfied.

Blessed are you who weep now, for you will

laugh.

너희 가난한 자는 복이 있나니 하나님의 나라가 너희 것임이요
지금 주린 자는 복이 있나니 너희가 배부름을 얻을 것임이요
지금 우는 자는 복이 있나니 너희가 웃을 것임이요 누가복음 6:20-21

DAY 23

If someone slaps you on one cheek, turn to them the other also. If someone takes your coat, do not withhold your shirt from them. Luke 6:29

If someone slaps you on one cheek, turn to

them the other also. If someone takes your

coat, do not withhold your shirt from them.

너의 이 뺨을 치는 자에게 저 뺨도 돌려대며 네 겉옷을 빼앗는 자에게 속옷도 거절하지 말라
누가복음 6:29

60

But love your enemies, do good to them, and lend to them without expecting to get anything back. Then your reward will be great, and you will be children of the Most High, because he is kind to the ungrateful and wicked. Luke 6:35

But love your enemies, do good to them, and lend to them without expecting to get anything back. Then your reward will be great, and you will be children of the Most High, because he is kind to the ungrateful and wicked.

오직 너희는 원수를 사랑하고 선대하며 아무 것도 바라지 말고 꾸어 주라 그리하면 너희 상이 클 것이요 또 지극히 높으신 이의 아들이 되리니 그는 은혜를 모르는 자와 악한 자에게도 인자하시니라 누가복음 6:35

Do not judge, and you will not be judged. Do not condemn, and you will not be condemned. Forgive, and you will be forgiven. Luke 6:37

Do not judge, and you will not be judged.

Do not condemn, and you will not be

condemned. Forgive, and you will be forgiven.

비판하지 말라 그리하면 너희가 비판을 받지 않을 것이요
정죄하지 말라 그리하면 너희가 정죄를 받지 않을 것이요
용서하라 그리하면 너희가 용서를 받을 것이요 누가복음 6:37

Jesus said to the woman, "Your faith has saved you; go in peace." Luke 7:50

Jesus said to the woman, "Your faith has saved you; go in peace."

예수께서 여자에게 이르시되
네 믿음이 너를 구원하였으니 평안히 가라 하시니라
누가복음 7:50

For whoever wants to save their life will lose it, but whoever loses their life for me will save it. What good is it for someone to gain the whole world, and yet lose or forfeit their very self? Luke 9:24-25

For whoever wants to save their life will lose it, but whoever loses their life for me will save it. What good is it for someone to gain the whole world, and yet lose or forfeit their very self?

누구든지 제 목숨을 구원하고자 하면 잃을 것이요
누구든지 나를 위하여 제 목숨을 잃으면 구원하리라
사람이 만일 온 천하를 얻고도 자기를 잃든지 빼앗기든지 하면 무엇이 유익하리요
누가복음 9:24-25

You also must be ready, because the Son of Man will come at an hour when you do not expect him. Luke 12:40

You also must be ready, because the Son of

Man will come at an hour when you do not

expect him.

그러므로 너희도 준비하고 있으라
생각하지 않은 때에 인자가 오리라 하시니라 누가복음 12:40

70

I tell you that in the same way there will be more rejoicing in heaven over one sinner who repents than over ninety-nine righteous persons who do not need to repent. Luke 15:7

I tell you that in the same way there will

be more rejoicing in heaven over one sinner

who repents than over ninety-nine righteous

persons who do not need to repent.

내가 너희에게 이르노니 이와 같이 죄인 한 사람이 회개하면
하늘에서는 회개할 것 없는 의인 아흔아홉으로 말미암아
기뻐하는 것보다 더하리라 누가복음 15:7

Whoever can be trusted with very little can also be trusted with much, and whoever is dishonest with very little will also be dishonest with much. Luke 16:10

Whoever can be trusted with very little can

also be trusted with much, and whoever

is dishonest with very little will also be

dishonest with much.

지극히 작은 것에 충성된 자는 큰 것에도 충성되고
지극히 작은 것에 불의한 자는 큰 것에도 불의하니라 누가복음 16:10

DAY 31

In the beginning was the Word, and the Word was with God, and the Word was God. John 1:1

In the beginning was the Word, and the Word was with God, and the Word was God.

태초에 말씀이 계시니라 이 말씀이 하나님과 함께 계셨으니
이 말씀은 곧 하나님이시니라 요한복음 1:1

The next day John saw Jesus coming toward him and said, "Look, the Lamb of God, who takes away the sin of the world!" John 1:29

The next day John saw Jesus coming toward him and said, "Look, the Lamb of God, who takes away the sin of the world!"

이튿날 요한이 예수께서 자기에게 나아오심을 보고 이르되
보라 세상 죄를 지고 가는 하나님의 어린 양이로다 요한복음 1:29

For God so loved the world that he gave his one and only Son, that whoever believes in him shall not perish but have eternal life. For God did not send his Son into the world to condemn the world, but to save the world through him. John 3:16-17

For God so loved the world that he gave his one and only Son, that whoever believes in him shall not perish but have eternal life. For God did not send his Son into the world to condemn the world, but to save the world through him.

하나님이 세상을 이처럼 사랑하사 독생자를 주셨으니
이는 그를 믿는 자마다 멸망하지 않고 영생을 얻게 하려 하심이라
하나님이 그 아들을 세상에 보내신 것은 세상을 심판하려 하심이 아니요
그로 말미암아 세상이 구원을 받게 하려 하심이라 요한복음 3:16-17

I am the good shepherd; I know my sheep and my sheep know me-just as the Father knows me and I know the Father-and I lay down my life for the sheep.

John 10:14-15

I am the good shepherd; I know my sheep

and my sheep know me-just as the Father

knows me and I know the Father-and I lay

down my life for the sheep.

나는 선한 목자라 나는 내 양을 알고 양도 나를 아는 것이
아버지께서 나를 아시고 내가 아버지를 아는 것 같으니
나는 양을 위하여 목숨을 버리노라 요한복음 10:14-15

Jesus said to her, "I am the resurrection and the life. The one who believes in me will live, even though they die; and whoever lives by believing in me will never die. Do you believe this?" John 11:25-26

Jesus said to her, "I am the resurrection and the life. The one who believes in me will live, even though they die; and whoever lives by believing in me will never die. Do you believe this?"

예수께서 이르시되 나는 부활이요 생명이니 나를 믿는 자는 죽어도 살겠고
무릇 살아서 나를 믿는 자는 영원히 죽지 아니하리니 이것을 네가 믿느냐
요한복음 11:25-26

"Yes, Lord," she replied, "I believe that you are the Messiah, the Son of God, who is to come into the world." John 11:27

"Yes, Lord," she replied, "I believe that you are the Messiah, the Son of God, who is to come into the world."

이르되 주여 그러하외다 주는 그리스도시요
세상에 오시는 하나님의 아들이신 줄 내가 믿나이다
요한복음 11:27

A new command I give you: Love one another. As I have loved you, so you must love one another. By this everyone will know that you are my disciples, if you love one another. John 13:34-35

A new command I give you: Love one another. As I have loved you, so you must love one another. By this everyone will know that you are my disciples, if you love one another.

새 계명을 너희에게 주노니 서로 사랑하라 내가 너희를 사랑한 것 같이 너희도 서로 사랑하라 너희가 서로 사랑하면 이로써 모든 사람이 너희가 내 제자인 줄 알리라 요한복음 13:34-35

Jesus answered, "I am the way and the truth and the life. No one comes to the Father except through me. If you really know me, you will know my Father as well. From now on, you do know him and have seen him." John 14 : 6-7

Jesus answered, "I am the way and the truth and the life. No one comes to the Father except through me. If you really know me, you will know my Father as well. From now on, you do know him and have seen him."

예수께서 이르시되 내가 곧 길이요 진리요 생명이니 나로 말미암지 않고는 아버지께로 올 자가 없느니라
너희가 나를 알았더라면 내 아버지도 알았으리로다 이제부터는 너희가 그를 알았고 또 보았느니라
요한복음 14:6-7

Peace I leave with you; my peace I give you. I do not give to you as the world gives. Do not let your hearts be troubled and do not be afraid. John 14:27

Peace I leave with you; my peace I give you. I do not give to you as the world gives. Do not let your hearts be troubled and do not be afraid.

평안을 너희에게 끼치노니 곧 나의 평안을 너희에게 주노라
내가 너희에게 주는 것은 세상이 주는 것과 같지 아니하니라
너희는 마음에 근심하지도 말고 두려워하지도 말라 요한복음 14:27

Then Jesus told him, "Because you have seen me, you have believed; blessed are those who have not seen and yet have believed." John 20:29

Then Jesus told him, "Because you have seen me, you have believed; blessed are those who have not seen and yet have believed."

예수께서 이르시되 너는 나를 본 고로 믿느냐
보지 못하고 믿는 자들은 복되도다 하시니라
요한복음 20:29

DAY 41~ DAY 60

• 사도행전·로마서·고린도전서
고린도후서·갈라디아서에서 뽑은 성경 구절

DAY 41

"In the last days," God says, "I will pour out my Spirit on all people. Your sons and daughters will prophesy, your young men will see visions, your old men will dream dreams." Acts 2:17

"In the last days," God says, "I will pour out my Spirit on all people. Your sons and daughters will prophesy, your young men will see visions, your old men will dream dreams."

하나님이 말씀하시기를 말세에 내가 내 영을 모든 육체에 부어 주리니 너희의 자녀들은 예언할 것이요 너희의 젊은이들은 환상을 보고 너희의 늙은이들은 꿈을 꾸리라 사도행전 2:17

Peter replied, "Repent and be baptized, every one of you, in the name of Jesus Christ for the forgiveness of your sins. And you will receive the gift of the Holy Spirit." Acts 2:38

Peter replied, "Repent and be baptized, every one of you, in the name of Jesus Christ for the forgiveness of your sins. And you will receive the gift of the Holy Spirit."

베드로가 이르되 너희가 회개하여 각각 예수 그리스도의 이름으로 세례를 받고 죄 사함을 받으라 그리하면 성령의 선물을 받으리니 사도행전 2:38

The following night the Lord stood near Paul and said, "Take courage! As you have testified about me in Jerusalem, so you must also testify in Rome."

Acts 23:11

The following night the Lord stood near Paul and said, "Take courage! As you have testified about me in Jerusalem, so you must also testify in Rome."

그 날 밤에 주께서 바울 곁에 서서 이르시되 담대하라 네가 예루살렘에서 나의 일을 증언한 것 같이 로마에서도 증언하여야 하리라 하시니라
사도행전 23:11

Very rarely will anyone die for a righteous person, though for a good person someone might possibly dare to die. But God demonstrates his own love for us in this: While we were still sinners, Christ died for us. Romans 5:7-8

Very rarely will anyone die for a righteous person, though for a good person someone might possibly dare to die. But God demonstrates his own love for us in this: While we were still sinners, Christ died for us.

의인을 위하여 죽는 자가 쉽지 않고 선인을 위하여 용감히 죽는 자가 혹 있거니와 우리가 아직 죄인 되었을 때에 그리스도께서 우리를 위하여 죽으심으로 하나님께서 우리에 대한 자기의 사랑을 확증하셨느니라 로마서 5:7-8

And we know that in all things God works for the good of those who love him, who have been called according to his purpose. Romans 8:28

And we know that in all things God works for the good of those who love him, who have been called according to his purpose.

우리가 알거니와 하나님을 사랑하는 자 곧 그의 뜻대로 부르심을 입은 자들에게는 모든 것이 합력하여 선을 이루느니라 로마서 8:28

Therefore, I urge you, brothers and sisters, in view of God's mercy, to offer your bodies as a living sacrifice, holy and pleasing to God-this is your true and proper worship. Romans 12:1

Therefore, I urge you, brothers and sisters, in view of God's mercy, to offer your bodies as a living sacrifice, holy and pleasing to God-this is your true and proper worship.

그러므로 형제들아 내가 하나님의 모든 자비하심으로 너희를 권하노니 너희 몸을
하나님이 기뻐하시는 거룩한 산 제물로 드리라 이는 너희가 드릴 영적 예배니라
로마서 12:1

DAY 47

Love must be sincere. Hate what is evil; cling to what is good. Romans 12:9

Love must be sincere. Hate what is evil;

cling to what is good.

사랑에는 거짓이 없나니 악을 미워하고 선에 속하라
로마서 12:9

DAY 48

May the God of hope fill you with all joy and peace as you trust in him, so that you may overflow with hope by the power of the Holy Spirit. Romans 15:13

May the God of hope fill you with all joy and peace as you trust in him, so that you may overflow with hope by the power of the Holy Spirit.

소망의 하나님이 모든 기쁨과 평강을 믿음 안에서 너희에게 충만하게 하사
성령의 능력으로 소망이 넘치게 하시기를 원하노라 로마서 15:13

I planted the seed, Apollos watered it, but God has been making it grow. So neither the one who plants nor the one who waters is anything, but only God, who makes things grow. 1 Corinthians 3:6-7

I planted the seed, Apollos watered it, but God has been making it grow. So neither the one who plants nor the one who waters is anything, but only God, who makes things grow.

나는 심었고 아볼로는 물을 주었으되 오직 하나님께서 자라나게 하셨나니
그런즉 심는 이나 물 주는 이는 아무 것도 아니로되 오직 자라게 하시는 이는 하나님뿐이니라
고린도전서 3:6-7

No temptation has overtaken you except what is common to mankind. And God is faithful; he will not let you be tempted beyond what you can bear. But when you are tempted, he will also provide a way out so that you can endure it. 1 Corinthians 10:13

No temptation has overtaken you except

what is common to mankind. And God

is faithful; he will not let you be tempted

beyond what you can bear. But when you

are tempted, he will also provide a way out

so that you can endure it.

사람이 감당할 시험 밖에는 너희가 당한 것이 없나니
오직 하나님은 미쁘사 너희가 감당하지 못할 시험 당함을 허락하지 아니하시고
시험 당할 즈음에 또한 피할 길을 내사 너희로 능히 감당하게 하시느니라
고린도전서 10:13

Love is patient, love is kind. It does not envy, it does not boast, it is not proud. It does not dishonor others, it is not self-seeking, it is not easily angered, it keeps no record of wrongs. 1 Corinthians 13 : 4-5

Love is patient, love is kind. It does not envy, it does not boast, it is not proud. It does not dishonor others, it is not self-seeking, it is not easily angered, it keeps no record of wrongs.

사랑은 오래 참고 사랑은 온유하며 시기하지 아니하며 사랑은 자랑하지 아니하며 교만하지 아니하며
무례히 행하지 아니하며 자기의 유익을 구하지 아니하며 성내지 아니하며 악한 것을 생각하지 아니하며
고린도전서 13:4-5

Love does not delight in evil but rejoices with the truth. It always protects, always trusts, always hopes, always perseveres. 1 Corinthians 13:6-7

Love does not delight in evil but rejoices with the truth. It always protects, always trusts, always hopes, always perseveres.

사랑은 불의를 기뻐하지 아니하며 진리와 함께 기뻐하고 모든 것을 참으며 모든 것을 믿으며 모든 것을 바라며 모든 것을 견디느니라 고린도전서 13:6-7

And now these three remain: faith, hope and love. But the greatest of these is love. 1 Corinthians 13:13

And now these three remain: faith, hope and love. But the greatest of these is love.

그런즉 믿음, 소망, 사랑, 이 세 가지는 항상 있을 것인데 그 중의 제일은 사랑이라
고린도전서 13:13

For our light and momentary troubles are achieving for us an eternal glory that far outweighs them all. So we fix our eyes not on what is seen, but on what is unseen, since what is seen is temporary, but what is unseen is eternal. 2 Corinthians 4 : 17-18

For our light and momentary troubles are

achieving for us an eternal glory that far

outweighs them all. So we fix our eyes not

on what is seen, but on what is unseen,

since what is seen is temporary, but what

is unseen is eternal.

우리가 잠시 받는 환난의 경한 것이 지극히 크고 영원한 영광의 중한 것을 우리에게 이루게 함이니
우리가 주목하는 것은 보이는 것이 아니요 보이지 않는 것이니 보이는 것은 잠깐이요
보이지 않는 것은 영원함이라 고린도후서 4:17-18

Therefore we are always confident and know that as long as we are at home in the body we are away from the Lord. For we live by faith, not by sight. 2 Corinthians 5:6-7

Therefore we are always confident and know that as long as we are at home in the body we are away from the Lord. For we live by faith, not by sight.

그러므로 우리가 항상 담대하여 몸으로 있을 때에는 주와 따로 있는 줄을 아노니
이는 우리가 믿음으로 행하고 보는 것으로 행하지 아니함이로라
고린도후서 5:6-7

DAY 56

So from now on we regard no one from a worldly point of view. Though we once regarded Christ in this way, we do so no longer. Therefore, if anyone is in Christ, the new creation has come: The old has gone, the new is here! 2 Corinthians 5:16-17

So from now on we regard no one from a worldly point of view. Though we once regarded Christ in this way, we do so no longer. Therefore, if anyone is in Christ, the new creation has come: The old has gone, the new is here!

그러므로 우리가 이제부터는 어떤 사람도 육신을 따라 알지 아니하노라
비록 우리가 그리스도도 육신을 따라 알았으나 이제부터는 그같이 알지 아니하노라
그런즉 누구든지 그리스도 안에 있으면 새로운 피조물이라
이전 것은 지나갔으니 보라 새 것이 되었도다 고린도후서 5:16-17

I have been crucified with Christ and I no longer live, but Christ lives in me. The life I now live in the body, I live by faith in the Son of God, who loved me and gave himself for me. Galatians 2:20

I have been crucified with Christ and I no longer live, but Christ lives in me. The life I now live in the body, I live by faith in the Son of God, who loved me and gave himself for me.

내가 그리스도와 함께 십자가에 못 박혔나니 그런즉 이제는 내가 사는 것이 아니요
오직 내 안에 그리스도께서 사시는 것이라 이제 내가 육체 가운데 사는 것은
나를 사랑하사 나를 위하여 자기 자신을 버리신 하나님의 아들을 믿는 믿음 안에서 사는 것이라
갈라디아서 2:20

Because you are his sons, God sent the Spirit of his Son into our hearts, the Spirit who calls out, "Abba, Father." Galatians 4:6

Because you are his sons, God sent the Spirit of his Son into our hearts, the Spirit who calls out, "Abba, Father."

너희가 아들이므로 하나님이 그 아들의 영을 우리 마음 가운데 보내사
아빠 아버지라 부르게 하셨느니라 갈라디아서 4:6

But the fruit of the Spirit is love, joy, peace, forbearance, kindness, goodness, faithfulness, gentleness and self-control. Against such things there is no law. Galatians 5:22-23

But the fruit of the Spirit is love, joy, peace, forbearance, kindness, goodness, faithfulness, gentleness and self-control. Against such things there is no law.

오직 성령의 열매는 사랑과 희락과 화평과 오래 참음과 자비와 양선과 충성과 온유와 절제니 이같은 것을 금지할 법이 없느니라 갈라디아서 5:22-23

May I never boast except in the cross of our Lord Jesus Christ, through which the world has been crucified to me, and I to the world. Galatians 6:14

May I never boast except in the cross of our Lord Jesus Christ, through which the world has been crucified to me, and I to the world.

그러나 내게는 우리 주 예수 그리스도의 십자가 외에 결코 자랑할 것이 없으니
그리스도로 말미암아 세상이 나를 대하여 십자가에 못 박히고 내가 또한 세상을 대하여 그러하니라
갈라디아서 6:14

• 에베소서 · 빌립보서 · 골로새서 · 데살로니가전서
데살로니가후서 · 디모데전서 · 디모데후서 · 디도서
빌레몬서 · 히브리서에서 뽑은 성경 구절

DAY 61

For it is by grace you have been saved, through faith-
and this not from yourselves, it is the gift of God-not
by works, so that no one can boast. Ephesians 2:8-9

For it is by grace you have been saved,

through faith-and this not from yourselves,

it is the gift of God-not by works, so that

no one can boast.

너희는 그 은혜에 의하여 믿음으로 말미암아 구원을 받았으니
이것은 너희에게서 난 것이 아니요 하나님의 선물이라
행위에서 난 것이 아니니 이는 누구든지 자랑하지 못하게 함이라
에베소서 2:8-9

140

In him and through faith in him we may approach God with freedom and confidence. I ask you, therefore, not to be discouraged because of my sufferings for you, which are your glory. Ephesians 3:12-13

In him and through faith in him we may approach God with freedom and confidence. I ask you, therefore, not to be discouraged because of my sufferings for you, which are your glory.

우리가 그 안에서 그를 믿음으로 말미암아 담대함과 확신을 가지고 하나님께 나아감을 얻느니라
그러므로 너희에게 구하노니 너희를 위한 나의 여러 환난에 대하여 낙심하지 말라 이는 너희의 영광이니라
에베소서 3:12-13

There is one body and one Spirit, just as you were called to one hope when you were called; one Lord, one faith, one baptism; one God and Father of all, who is over all and through all and in all. Ephesians 4 : 4-6

There is one body and one Spirit, just as you were called to one hope when you were called; one Lord, one faith, one baptism; one God and Father of all, who is over all and through all and in all.

몸이 하나요 성령도 한 분이시니 이와 같이 너희가 부르심의 한 소망 안에서 부르심을 받았느니라
주도 한 분이시요 믿음도 하나요 세례도 하나요
하나님도 한 분이시니 곧 만유의 아버지시라 만유 위에 계시고 만유를 통일하시고 만유 가운데 계시도다
에베소서 4:4-6

In all my prayers for all of you, I always pray with joy because of your partnership in the gospel from the first day until now, being confident of this, that he who began a good work in you will carry it on to completion until the day of Christ Jesus. Philippians 1:4-6

In all my prayers for all of you, I always pray with joy because of your partnership in the gospel from the first day until now, being confident of this, that he who began a good work in you will carry it on to completion until the day of Christ Jesus.

간구할 때마다 너희 무리를 위하여 기쁨으로 항상 간구함은
너희가 첫날부터 이제까지 복음을 위한 일에 참여하고 있기 때문이라
너희 안에서 착한 일을 시작하신 이가 그리스도 예수의 날까지 이루실 줄을 우리는 확신하노라
빌립보서 1:4-6

Convinced of this, I know that I will remain, and I will continue with all of you for your progress and joy in the faith, so that through my being with you again your boasting in Christ Jesus will abound on account of me. Philippians 1:25-26

Convinced of this, I know that I will

remain, and I will continue with all of you

for your progress and joy in the faith, so

that through my being with you again your

boasting in Christ Jesus will abound on

account of me.

내가 살 것과 너희 믿음의 진보와 기쁨을 위하여 너희 무리와 함께 거할 이것을 확실히 아노니
내가 다시 너희와 같이 있음으로 그리스도 예수 안에서 너희 자랑이 나로 말미암아 풍성하게 하려 함이라
빌립보서 1:25-26

Who, being in very nature God, did not consider equality with God something to be used to his own advantage; rather, he made himself nothing by taking the very nature of a servant, being made in human likeness. Philippians 2:6-7

Who, being in very nature God, did not consider equality with God something to be used to his own advantage; rather, he made himself nothing by taking the very nature of a servant, being made in human likeness.

그는 근본 하나님의 본체시나 하나님과 동등됨을 취할 것으로 여기지 아니하시고
오히려 자기를 비워 종의 형체를 가지사 사람들과 같이 되셨고
빌립보서 2:6-7

And being found in appearance as a man, he humbled himself by becoming obedient to death- even death on a cross! Philippians 2:8

And being found in appearance as a man, he

humbled himself by becoming obedient to death

even death on a cross!

사람의 모양으로 나타나사 자기를 낮추시고 죽기까지 복종하셨으니 곧 십자가에 죽으심이라
빌립보서 2:8

Finally, brothers and sisters, whatever is true, whatever is noble, whatever is right, whatever is pure, whatever is lovely, whatever is admirable-if anything is excellent or praiseworthy-think about such things. Philippians 4:8

Finally, brothers and sisters, whatever is

true, whatever is noble, whatever is right,

whatever is pure, whatever is lovely,

whatever is admirable- if anything is excellent

or praiseworthy- think about such things.

끝으로 형제들아 무엇에든지 참되며 무엇에든지 경건하며 무엇에든지 옳으며
무엇에든지 정결하며 무엇에든지 사랑 받을 만하며 무엇에든지 칭찬 받을 만하며
무슨 덕이 있든지 무슨 기림이 있든지 이것들을 생각하라
빌립보서 4:8

I know what it is to be in need, and I know what it is to have plenty. I have learned the secret of being content in any and every situation, whether well fed or hungry, whether living in plenty or in want. I can do all this through him who gives me strength. Philippians 4:12-13

I know what it is to be in need, and I know what it is to have plenty. I have learned the secret of being content in any and every situation, whether well fed or hungry, whether living in plenty or in want. I can do all this through him who gives me strength.

나는 비천에 처할 줄도 알고 풍부에 처할 줄도 알아
모든 일 곧 배부름과 배고픔과 풍부와 궁핍에도 처할 줄 아는
일체의 비결을 배웠노라
내게 능력 주시는 자 안에서 내가 모든 것을 할 수 있느니라 빌립보서 4:12-13

So then, just as you received Christ Jesus as Lord, continue to live your lives in him, rooted and built up in him, strengthened in the faith as you were taught, and overflowing with thankfulness. Colossians 2:6-7

So then, just as you received Christ Jesus as

Lord, continue to live your lives in him,

rooted and built up in him, strengthened in

the faith as you were taught, and overflowing

with thankfulness.

그러므로 너희가 그리스도 예수를 주로 받았으니 그 안에서 행하되
그 안에 뿌리를 박으며 세움을 받아 교훈을 받은 대로 믿음에 굳게 서서 감사함을 넘치게 하라
골로새서 2:6-7

DAY 71

Rejoice always, pray continually, give thanks in all circumstances; for this is God's will for you in Christ Jesus. 1 Thessalonians 5:16-18

Rejoice always, pray continually, give thanks in all circumstances; for this is God's will for you in Christ Jesus.

항상 기뻐하라
쉬지 말고 기도하라
범사에 감사하라
이것이 그리스도 예수 안에서 너희를 향하신 하나님의 뜻이니라
데살로니가전서 5:16-18

But we ought always to thank God for you, brothers and sisters loved by the Lord, because God chose you as firstfruits to be saved through the sanctifying work of the Spirit and through belief in the truth.

2 Thessalonians 2:13

But we ought always to thank God for

you, brothers and sisters loved by the Lord,

because God chose you as firstfruits to be

saved through the sanctifying work of the

Spirit and through belief in the truth.

주께서 사랑하시는 형제들아 우리가 항상 너희에 관하여 마땅히 하나님께 감사할 것은
하나님이 처음부터 너희를 택하사 성령의 거룩하게 하심과
진리를 믿음으로 구원을 받게 하심이니 데살로니가후서 2:13

For there is one God and one mediator between God and mankind, the man Christ Jesus, who gave himself as a ransom for all people. This has now been witnessed to at the proper time. 1 Timothy 2:5-6

For there is one God and one mediator between God and mankind, the man Christ Jesus, who gave himself as a ransom for all people. This has now been witnessed to at the proper time.

하나님은 한 분이시요 또 하나님과 사람 사이에 중보자도 한 분이시니 곧 사람이신 그리스도 예수라 그가 모든 사람을 위하여 자기를 대속물로 주셨으니 기약이 이르러 주신 증거니라
디모데전서 2:5-6

All Scripture is God-breathed and is useful for teaching, rebuking, correcting and training in righteousness, so that the servant of God may be thoroughly equipped for every good work. 2 Timothy 3:16-17

All Scripture is God-breathed and is

useful for teaching, rebuking, correcting and

training in righteousness, so that the servant

of God may be thoroughly equipped for every

good work.

모든 성경은 하나님의 감동으로 된 것으로 교훈과 책망과 바르게 함과 의로 교육하기에 유익하니
이는 하나님의 사람으로 온전하게 하며 모든 선한 일을 행할 능력을 갖추게 하려 함이라
디모데후서 3:16-17

Jesus Christ who gave himself for us to redeem us from all wickedness and to purify for himself a people that are his very own, eager to do what is good. Titus 2:14

Jesus Christ who gave himself for us to redeem us from all wickedness and to purify for himself a people that are his very own, eager to do what is good.

그가 우리를 대신하여 자신을 주심은 모든 불법에서 우리를 속량하시고
우리를 깨끗하게 하사 선한 일을 열심히 하는 자기 백성이 되게 하려 하심이라
디도서 2:14

I do wish, brother, that I may have some benefit from you in the Lord; refresh my heart in Christ. Confident of your obedience, I write to you, knowing that you will do even more than I ask. Philemon 1:20-21

I do wish, brother, that I may have some benefit from you in the Lord; refresh my heart in Christ. Confident of your obedience, I write to you, knowing that you will do even more than I ask.

오 형제여 나로 주 안에서 너로 말미암아 기쁨을 얻게 하고
내 마음이 그리스도 안에서 평안하게 하라
나는 네가 순종할 것을 확신하므로 네게 썼노니
네가 내가 말한 것보다 더 행할 줄을 아노라 빌레몬서 1:20-21

Son though he was, he learned obedience from what he suffered and, once made perfect, he became the source of eternal salvation for all who obey him and was designated by God to be high priest in the order of Melchizedek. Hebrews 5:8-10

Son though he was, he learned obedience from what he suffered and, once made perfect, he became the source of eternal salvation for all who obey him and was designated by God to be high priest in the order of Melchizedek.

그가 아들이시면서도 받으신 고난으로 순종함을 배워서
온전하게 되셨은즉 자기에게 순종하는 모든 자에게 영원한 구원의 근원이 되시고
하나님께 멜기세덱의 반차를 따른 대제사장이라 칭하심을 받으셨느니라
히브리서 5:8-10

Now faith is confidence in what we hope for and assurance about what we do not see. This is what the ancients were commended for. Hebrews 11:1-2

Now faith is confidence in what we hope for

and assurance about what we do not see. This

is what the ancients were commended for.

믿음은 바라는 것들의 실상이요 보이지 않는 것들의 증거니
선진들이 이로써 증거를 얻었느니라 히브리서 11:1-2

Fixing our eyes on Jesus, the pioneer and perfecter of faith. For the joy set before him he endured the cross, scorning its shame, and sat down at the right hand of the throne of God. Hebrews 12:2

Fixing our eyes on Jesus, the pioneer and perfecter of faith. For the joy set before him he endured the cross, scorning its shame, and sat down at the right hand of the throne of God.

믿음의 주요 또 온전하게 하시는 이인 예수를 바라보자 그는 그 앞에 있는 기쁨을 위하여 십자가를 참으사 부끄러움을 개의치 아니하시더니 하나님 보좌 우편에 앉으셨느니라 히브리서 12:2

Remember your leaders, who spoke the word of God to you. Consider the outcome of their way of life and imitate their faith. Jesus Christ is the same yesterday and today and forever. Hebrews 13:7-8

Remember your leaders, who spoke the word of God to you. Consider the outcome of their way of life and imitate their faith. Jesus Christ is the same yesterday and today and forever.

하나님의 말씀을 너희에게 일러 주고 너희를 인도하던 자들을 생각하며
그들의 행실의 결말을 주의하여 보고 그들의 믿음을 본받으라
예수 그리스도는 어제나 오늘이나 영원토록 동일하시니라
히브리서 13:7-8

• 야고보서 · 베드로전서 · 베드로후서
요한1서 · 요한2서 · 요한3서 · 유다서
요한계시록에서 뽑은 성경 구절

Consider it pure joy, my brothers and sisters, whenever you face trials of many kinds, because you know that the testing of your faith produces perseverance. James 1:2-3

Consider it pure joy, my brothers and sisters,

whenever you face trials of many kinds,

because you know that the testing of your

faith produces perseverance.

내 형제들아 너희가 여러 가지 시험을 당하거든 온전히 기쁘게 여기라
이는 너희 믿음의 시련이 인내를 만들어 내는 줄 너희가 앎이라
야고보서 1:2-3

If any of you lacks wisdom, you should ask God, who gives generously to all without finding fault, and it will be given to you. James 1:5

If any of you lacks wisdom, you should ask God, who gives generously to all without finding fault, and it will be given to you.

너희 중에 누구든지 지혜가 부족하거든 모든 사람에게 후히 주시고
꾸짖지 아니하시는 하나님께 구하라 그리하면 주시리라
야고보서 1:5

Blessed is the one who perseveres under trial because, having stood the test, that person will receive the crown of life that the Lord has promised to those who love him. James 1:12

Blessed is the one who perseveres under trial

because, having stood the test, that person

will receive the crown of life that the Lord

has promised to those who love him.

시험을 참는 자는 복이 있나니 이는 시련을 견디어 낸 자가 주께서 자기를
사랑하는 자들에게 약속하신 생명의 면류관을 얻을 것이기 때문이라
야고보서 1:12

My dear brothers and sisters, take note of this: Everyone should be quick to listen, slow to speak and slow to become angry. James 1:19

My dear brothers and sisters, take note of this: Everyone should be quick to listen, slow to speak and slow to become angry.

내 사랑하는 형제들아 너희가 알지니 사람마다 듣기는 속히 하고 말하기는 더디 하며 성내기도 더디 하라 야고보서 1:19

Why, you do not even know what will happen tomorrow. What is your life? You are a mist that appears for a little while and then vanishes. James 4 : 14

Why, you do not even know what will

happen tomorrow. What is your life? You

are a mist that appears for a little while and

then vanishes.

내일 일을 너희가 알지 못하는도다 너희 생명이 무엇이냐
너희는 잠깐 보이다가 없어지는 안개니라 야고보서 4:14

The end of all things is near. Therefore be alert and of sober mind so that you may pray. Above all, love each other deeply, because love covers over a multitude of sins. 1 Peter 4:7-8

The end of all things is near. Therefore be alert and of sober mind so that you may pray. Above all, love each other deeply, because love covers over a multitude of sins.

만물의 마지막이 가까이 왔으니 그러므로 너희는 정신을 차리고 근신하여 기도하라
무엇보다도 뜨겁게 서로 사랑할지니 사랑은 허다한 죄를 덮느니라
베드로전서 4:7-8

But do not forget this one thing, dear friends:
With the Lord a day is like a thousand years, and a
thousand years are like a day. 2 Peter 3:8

But do not forget this one thing, dear friends :

With the Lord a day is like a thousand

years, and a thousand years are like a day.

사랑하는 자들아 주께는 하루가 천 년 같고 천 년이 하루 같다는
이 한 가지를 잊지 말라 베드로후서 3:8

The Lord is not slow in keeping his promise, as some understand slowness. Instead he is patient with you, not wanting anyone to perish, but everyone to come to repentance. 2 Peter 3:9

The Lord is not slow in keeping his promise,

as some understand slowness. Instead he is

patient with you, not wanting anyone to

perish, but everyone to come to repentance.

주의 약속은 어떤 이들이 더디다고 생각하는 것 같이 더딘 것이 아니라
오직 주께서는 너희를 대하여 오래 참으사 아무도 멸망하지 아니하고
다 회개하기에 이르기를 원하시느니라 베드로후서 3:9

If we confess our sins, he is faithful and just and will forgive us our sins and purify us from all unrighteousness. 1 John 1:9

If we confess our sins, he is faithful and just and will forgive us our sins and purify us from all unrighteousness.

만일 우리가 우리 죄를 자백하면 그는 미쁘시고 의로우사 우리 죄를 사하시며 우리를 모든 불의에서 깨끗하게 하실 것이요 요한1서 1:9

See what great love the Father has lavished on us, that we should be called children of God! And that is what we are! The reason the world does not know us is that it did not know him. 1 John 3:1

See what great love the Father has lavished on us, that we should be called children of God! And that is what we are! The reason the world does not know us is that it did not know him.

보라 아버지께서 어떠한 사랑을 우리에게 베푸사 하나님의 자녀라 일컬음을 받게 하셨는가 우리가 그러하도다 그러므로 세상이 우리를 알지 못함은 그를 알지 못함이라
요한1서 3:1

Dear children, let us not love with words or speech but with actions and in truth. 1 John 3:18

Dear children, let us not love with words or speech but with actions and in truth.

자녀들아 우리가 말과 혀로만 사랑하지 말고 행함과 진실함으로 하자
요한1서 3:18

Dear friends, let us love one another, for love comes from God. Everyone who loves has been born of God and knows God. Whoever does not love does not know God, because God is love. 1 John 4:7-8

Dear friends, let us love one another, for

love comes from God. Everyone who loves

has been born of God and knows God.

Whoever does not love does not know God,

because God is love.

사랑하는 자들아 우리가 서로 사랑하자 사랑은 하나님께 속한 것이니
사랑하는 자마다 하나님으로부터 나서 하나님을 알고
사랑하지 아니하는 자는 하나님을 알지 못하나니 이는 하나님은 사랑이심이라
요한1서 4:7-8

DAY 93

And so we know and rely on the love God has for us. God is love. Whoever lives in love lives in God, and God in them. 1 John 4:16

And so we know and rely on the love God has for us. God is love. Whoever lives in love lives in God, and God in them.

하나님이 우리를 사랑하시는 사랑을 우리가 알고 믿었노니 하나님은 사랑이시라
사랑 안에 거하는 자는 하나님 안에 거하고 하나님도 그의 안에 거하시느니라
요한1서 4:16

There is no fear in love. But perfect love drives out fear, because fear has to do with punishment. The one who fears is not made perfect in love. 1 John 4 : 18

There is no fear in love. But perfect love drives out fear, because fear has to do with punishment. The one who fears is not made perfect in love.

사랑 안에 두려움이 없고 온전한 사랑이 두려움을 내쫓나니 두려움에는 형벌이 있음이라 두려워하는 자는 사랑 안에서 온전히 이루지 못하였느니라 요한1서 4:18

Grace, mercy and peace from God the Father and from Jesus Christ, the Father's Son, will be with us in truth and love. 2 John 1:3

Grace, mercy and peace from God the Father and from Jesus Christ, the Father's Son, will be with us in truth and love.

은혜와 긍휼과 평강이 하나님 아버지와 아버지의 아들 예수 그리스도께로부터 진리와 사랑 가운데서 우리와 함께 있으리라 요한2서 1:3

I have no greater joy than to hear that my children are walking in the truth. 3 John 1:4

I have no greater joy than to hear that my

children are walking in the truth.

내가 내 자녀들이 진리 안에서 행한다 함을 듣는 것보다 더 기쁜 일이 없도다
요한3서 1:4

But you, dear friends, by building yourselves up in your most holy faith and praying in the Holy Spirit, keep yourselves in God's love as you wait for the mercy of our Lord Jesus Christ to bring you to eternal life. Jude 1:20-21

But you, dear friends, by building yourselves up in your most holy faith and praying in the Holy Spirit, keep yourselves in God's love as you wait for the mercy of our Lord Jesus Christ to bring you to eternal life.

사랑하는 자들아 너희는 너희의 지극히 거룩한 믿음 위에 자신을 세우며 성령으로 기도하며
하나님의 사랑 안에서 자신을 지키며 영생에 이르도록 우리 주 예수 그리스도의 긍휼을 기다리라
유다서 1:20-21

Here I am! I stand at the door and knock. If anyone hears my voice and opens the door, I will come in and eat with that person, and they with me. Revelation 3:20

Here I am! I stand at the door and knock.

If anyone hears my voice and opens the

door, I will come in and eat with that

person, and they with me.

볼지어다 내가 문 밖에 서서 두드리노니 누구든지 내 음성을 듣고 문을 열면
내가 그에게로 들어가 그와 더불어 먹고 그는 나와 더불어 먹으리라
요한계시록 3:20

To the one who is victorious, I will give the right to sit with me on my throne, just as I was victorious and sat down with my Father on his throne. Revelation 3:21

To the one who is victorious, I will give the

right to sit with me on my throne, just as I

was victorious and sat down with my Father

on his throne.

이기는 그에게는 내가 내 보좌에 함께 앉게 하여 주기를
내가 이기고 아버지 보좌에 함께 앉은 것과 같이 하리라 요한계시록 3:21

And when he had taken it, the four living creatures and the twenty-four elders fell down before the Lamb. Each one had a harp and they were holding golden bowls full of incense, which are the prayers of God's people. Revelation 5:8

And when he had taken it, the four living creatures and the twenty-four elders fell down before the Lamb. Each one had a harp and they were holding golden bowls full of incense, which are the prayers of God's people.

그 두루마리를 취하시매 네 생물과 이십사 장로들이 그 어린 양 앞에 엎드려 각각 거문고와 향이 가득한 금 대접을 가졌으니 이 향은 성도의 기도들이라
요한계시록 5:8

My favorite bible verse

좋아하는 성경 구절 쓰기

영어 필기체 10일 완성 노트 스프링 제본
영어 필기체 왕초보를 위한 기초 학습서

기획·구성 펜앤페이퍼(Pen&Paper) | 감수 이지(Izzie) | 가격 14,000원

영어 필기체 100일 기적의 노트 스프링 제본
섬세한 취향의 만년필 애호가를 위한 영어 필기체 필사 노트

기획·구성 펜앤페이퍼(Pen&Paper) | 감수 이지(Izzie) | 가격 26,000원

어린 왕자 영어 필기체 100일 필사 노트 스프링 제본
진실된 관계로 안내하는 《어린 왕자》의 명문장을 영어 필기체로 완성하는 노트

원저 앙투안 드 생텍쥐페리 | 구성 펜앤페이퍼 | 가격 17,800원

음악이 있는 팝송 영어 필사 따라 쓰며 배우는 인생 팝송
시적 표현, 아름다운 문장, 서정적인 멜로디가 담긴 명곡 필사 노트

기획·구성 펜앤페이퍼(Pen&Paper) | 감수 이지(Izzie) | 가격 16,800원

Anne of Green Gables 사철 제본
《빨강머리 앤》의 주요 이야기를 영어로 필사하는 책

글 루시 모드 몽고메리 | 가격 15,000원

The Little Prince 사철 제본
《어린 왕자》의 전문을 영어로 필사하는 책

글 앙투안드 드 생텍쥐페리 | 가격 15,000원

Alice's Adventures in Wonderland 사철 제본
《이상한 나라의 앨리스》의 전문을 영어로 필사하는 책

글 루이스 캐럴 | 가격 18,500원